I am so *grateful*

Sky Hawk

Published by Uiri Press 2016
First edition, first printing

Design and writing © 2016 Sky Hawk

Photo credit: photo credit: Muffet <a href="http://www.flickr.com/photos/53133240@N00/4233997846">firetex</a> via <a href="http://photopin.com">photopin</a> <a href="https://creativecommons.org/licenses/by/2.0/">(license)</a>

All rights reserved. No part of this book may be reproduced or transmitted in any form or by any means, including but not limited to information storage and retrieval systems, electronic, mechanical, photocopy, recording, etc. without written permission from the copyright holder.

ISBN; 978-0-9979051-1-3

Dedication

I am so appreciative to all the beautiful souls who take time to be thankful and loving.

How To Use This Book

This is a 42 day journal that is focused on cultivating more gratitude in your life!

1. Read the quote and get inspired. I like to use these for a daily focus.

2. Write down how you showed your gratitude to someone else. This could include telling someone how grateful you are or something that you physically did.

3. Write down at least three *different* things that you are thankful for. These can be little things like, I am thankful I found my umbrella, to big things like, I am so thankful that I got my dream job.

4. Try to get outside into Nature everyday and take a deep breath. Make a little sketch of what you are thankful for while there. It's OK to cut and paste pictures as well.

5. Take a moment to note anything unexpected that happened today that was good. As you focus on gratitude you may notice more and more of this happening.

6. Every seventh day there will be a weekly review. On the right hand page you will write a letter to someone who you need to thank. This may be from the past, present, or future. Then fill in the gratitude meter by shading in where you feel you are at. "I feel the stirrings of something new", is like a 0, "my heart is so welled up", is like a 10.

I showed my thanks to someone today by....

_____
_____
_____
_____
_____
_____
_____

Write down at least 3 things you feel gratitude for today.
As a personal challenge see if you can fill all the lines with things you feel thankful for.

_____
_____
_____
_____
_____
_____
_____
_____
_____
_____
_____
_____
_____

> *At times our own light goes out and is rekindled by a spark from another person. Each of us has cause to think with deep gratitude of those who have lighted the flame within us.*
> *Albert Schweitzer*

Something in Nature I feel grateful for

Unexpected goodness that happened today

_____
_____
_____
_____
_____
_____
_____
_____

I showed my thanks to someone today by....

_____
_____
_____
_____
_____
_____
_____
_____

Write down at least 3 things you feel gratitude for today. As a personal challenge see if you can fill all the lines with things you feel thankful for.

_____
_____
_____
_____
_____
_____
_____
_____
_____
_____
_____
_____

> *I wanted to say thanks... and share my gratitude for everything I've been blessed with. Family, friends, and continued support from everyone.*
> *Travis Barker*

Something in Nature I feel grateful for

Unexpected goodness that happened today.......

_____
_____
_____
_____
_____
_____

I showed my thanks to someone today by....

_____
_____
_____
_____
_____
_____
_____

Write down at least 3 things you feel gratitude for today.
As a personal challenge see if you can fill all the lines with things you feel thankful for.

_____
_____
_____
_____
_____
_____
_____
_____
_____
_____
_____
_____

> *Develop an attitude of gratitude, and give thanks for everything that happens to you, knowing that every step forward is a step toward achieving something bigger and better than your current situation.*
> *Brian Tracy*

Something in Nature I feel grateful for

Unexpected goodness that happened today

_____
_____
_____
_____
_____
_____
_____
_____

I showed my thanks to someone today by....

_____
_____
_____
_____
_____
_____
_____

Write down at least 3 things you feel gratitude for today. As a personal challenge see if you can fill all the lines with things you feel thankful for.

_____
_____
_____
_____
_____
_____
_____
_____
_____
_____

> *I write about gratitude because I am thankful - for all of it.*
> *Kristin Armstrong*

Something in Nature I feel grateful for

Unexpected goodness that happened today

_____
_____
_____
_____
_____
_____
_____
_____

I showed my thanks to someone today by....

_____
_____
_____
_____
_____
_____
_____
_____

Write down at least 3 things you feel gratitude for today.
As a personal challenge see if you can fill all the lines with things you feel thankful for.

_____
_____
_____
_____
_____
_____
_____
_____
_____
_____
_____

> *Gratitude can transform common days into thanksgivings, turn routine jobs into joy, and change ordinary opportunities into blessings.*
> William Arthur Ward

Something in Nature I feel grateful for

Unexpected goodness that happened today

_____
_____
_____
_____
_____
_____
_____
_____

I showed my thanks to someone today by....

_____
_____
_____
_____
_____
_____
_____

Write down at least 3 things you feel gratitude for today. As a personal challenge see if you can fill all the lines with things you feel thankful for.

_____
_____
_____
_____
_____
_____
_____
_____
_____
_____
_____
_____
_____

> *Gratitude unlocks the fullness of life. It turns what we have into enough, and more. It turns denial into acceptance, chaos to order, confusion to clarity. It can turn a meal into a feast, a house into a home, a stranger into a friend.*
> *Melody Beattie*

Something in Nature I feel grateful for

Unexpected goodness that happened today

What a week! I love my gratitude journal.

Write down the difference you notice in your life as you have been focused on gratitude.

_____
_____
_____
_____
_____
_____
_____
_____
_____
_____
_____
_____
_____
_____
_____

> *Gratitude is the fairest blossom which springs from the soul.*
> *Henry Ward Beecher*

**** *3 things I am grateful for today* ****

_____
_____
_____
_____
_____

Dear _____

I never got to properly thank you. I would like to do that now........

_____
_____
_____
_____
_____
_____
_____
_____
_____
_____
_____
_____
_____
_____
_____
_____
_____
_____
_____
_____
_____
_____

gratitude meter

I feel the stirrings of something new ┆ ┆ my heart is so welled up with gratitude

I showed my thanks to someone today by....

_____
_____
_____
_____
_____
_____
_____

Write down at least 3 things you feel gratitude for today. As a personal challenge see if you can fill all the lines with things you feel thankful for.

_____
_____
_____
_____
_____
_____
_____
_____
_____
_____
_____
_____

If having a soul means being able to feel love and loyalty and gratitude, then animals are better off than a lot of humans.
James Herriot

Something in Nature I feel grateful for

Unexpected goodness that happened today

_____
_____
_____
_____
_____
_____
_____
_____

I showed my thanks to someone today by....
_____
_____
_____
_____
_____
_____
_____

Write down at least 3 things you feel gratitude for today.
As a personal challenge see if you can fill all the lines with things you feel thankful for.

_____
_____
_____
_____
_____
_____
_____
_____
_____
_____
_____

> *The essence of all beautiful art, all great art, is gratitude.*
> *Friedrich Nietzsche*

Something in Nature I feel grateful for

Unexpected goodness that happened today

_____
_____
_____
_____
_____
_____
_____
_____

I showed my thanks to someone today by....

___

Write down at least 3 things you feel gratitude for today.
As a personal challenge see if you can fill all the lines with things you feel thankful for.

___

> *Joy is the simplest form of gratitude.*
> *Karl Barth*

Something in Nature I feel grateful for

Unexpected goodness that happened today

_____
_____
_____
_____
_____
_____
_____
_____

I showed my thanks to someone today by....

_____
_____
_____
_____
_____
_____
_____
_____

Write down at least 3 things you feel gratitude for today.
As a personal challenge see if you can fill all the lines with things you feel thankful for.

_____
_____
_____
_____
_____
_____
_____
_____
_____
_____
_____

> *Gratitude bestows reverence, allowing us to encounter everyday epiphanies, those transcendent moments of awe that change forever how we experience life and the world.*
> John Milton

Something in Nature I feel grateful for

Unexpected goodness that happened today

_____
_____
_____
_____
_____
_____
_____
_____

I showed my thanks to someone today by....

_____
_____
_____
_____
_____
_____
_____

Write down at least 3 things you feel gratitude for today.
As a personal challenge see if you can fill all the lines with things you feel thankful for.

_____
_____
_____
_____
_____
_____
_____
_____
_____
_____
_____
_____
_____

> *Gratitude is the healthiest of all human emotions. The more you express gratitude for what you have, the more likely you will have even more to express gratitude for. Zig Ziglar*

Something in Nature I feel grateful for

Unexpected goodness that happened today

I showed my thanks to someone today by....

_____
_____
_____
_____
_____
_____
_____
_____

Write down at least 3 things you feel gratitude for today. As a personal challenge see if you can fill all the lines with things you feel thankful for.

_____
_____
_____
_____
_____
_____
_____
_____
_____
_____
_____

> *Gratitude makes sense of our past, brings peace for today, and creates a vision for tomorrow.*
> *Melody Beattie*

Something in Nature I feel grateful for

Unexpected goodness that happened today

_____
_____
_____
_____
_____
_____
_____
_____

What a week! I love my gratitude journal.

Write down the difference you notice in your life as you have been focused on gratitude.

> *When we focus on our gratitude, the tide of disappointment goes out and the tide of love rushes in.*
> *Kristin Armstrong*

**** 3 things I am grateful for today ****

Dear _____
I never got to properly thank you. I would like to do that now........

_____
_____
_____
_____
_____
_____
_____
_____
_____
_____
_____
_____
_____
_____
_____
_____
_____
_____
_____
_____

gratitude meter

| I feel the stirrings of something new | | my heart is so welled up with gratitude |

I showed my thanks to someone today by....

Write down at least 3 things you feel gratitude for today.
As a personal challenge see if you can fill all the lines with things you feel thankful for.

Gratitude is not only the greatest of virtues, but the parent of all the others.
Marcus Tullius Cicero

Something in Nature I feel grateful for

Unexpected goodness that happened today

_____
_____
_____
_____
_____
_____
_____
_____

I showed my thanks to someone today by....

_____
_____
_____
_____
_____
_____
_____
_____

Write down at least 3 things you feel gratitude for today. As a personal challenge see if you can fill all the lines with things you feel thankful for.

_____
_____
_____
_____
_____
_____
_____
_____
_____
_____
_____

> *No one who achieves success does so without acknowledging the help of others. The wise and confident acknowledge this help with gratitude.*
> *Alfred North Whitehead*

Something in Nature I feel grateful for

Unexpected goodness that happened today

_____
_____
_____
_____
_____
_____
_____
_____

I showed my thanks to someone today by....

___

Write down at least 3 things you feel gratitude for today. As a personal challenge see if you can fill all the lines with things you feel thankful for.

___

> *Feeling gratitude and not expressing it is like wrapping a present and not giving it.*
> *William Arthur Ward*

Something in Nature I feel grateful for

Unexpected goodness that happened today

_____
_____
_____
_____
_____
_____
_____
_____

I showed my thanks to someone today by....

_____
_____
_____
_____
_____
_____
_____
_____

Write down at least 3 things you feel gratitude for today. As a personal challenge see if you can fill all the lines with things you feel thankful for.

_____
_____
_____
_____
_____
_____
_____
_____
_____
_____
_____
_____
_____
_____

> *It is through gratitude for the present moment that the spiritual dimension of life opens up.*
> *Eckhart Tolle*

Something in Nature I feel grateful for

Unexpected goodness that happened today

_____
_____
_____
_____
_____
_____
_____
_____
_____

I showed my thanks to someone today by....

_____
_____
_____
_____
_____
_____
_____
_____

Write down at least 3 things you feel gratitude for today.
As a personal challenge see if you can fill all the lines with things you feel thankful for.

_____
_____
_____
_____
_____
_____
_____
_____
_____
_____
_____

> *Gratitude helps you to grow and expand; gratitude brings joy and laughter into your life and into the lives of all those around you.*
> *Eileen Caddy*

Something in Nature I feel grateful for

Unexpected goodness that happened today

_____
_____
_____
_____
_____
_____
_____

I showed my thanks to someone today by....

_____
_____
_____
_____
_____
_____
_____

Write down at least 3 things you feel gratitude for today.
As a personal challenge see if you can fill all the lines with things you feel thankful for.

_____
_____
_____
_____
_____
_____
_____
_____
_____
_____
_____
_____

> *'Thank you' is the best prayer that anyone could say. I say that one a lot. Thank you expresses extreme gratitude, humility, understanding.*
> *Alice Walker*

Something in Nature I feel grateful for

Unexpected goodness that happened today

_____
_____
_____
_____
_____
_____
_____
_____
_____

What a week! I love my gratitude journal.

Write down the difference you notice in your life as you have been focused on gratitude.

___

> *Sometimes we should express our gratitude for the small and simple things like the scent of the rain, the taste of your favorite food, or the sound of a loved one's voice. Joseph B. Wirthlin*

**** 3 things I am grateful for today ****

Dear _____
I never got to properly thank you. I would like to do that now........

_____
_____
_____
_____
_____
_____
_____
_____
_____
_____
_____
_____
_____
_____
_____
_____
_____
_____
_____
_____

gratitude meter

I feel the stirrings of something new │ │ my heart is so welled up with gratitude

I showed my thanks to someone today by....
_____
_____
_____
_____
_____
_____
_____
_____

Write down at least 3 things you feel gratitude for today. As a personal challenge see if you can fill all the lines with things you feel thankful for.

_____
_____
_____
_____
_____
_____
_____
_____
_____
_____
_____
_____
_____

> *I don't have to chase extraordinary moments to find happiness - it's right in front of me if I'm paying attention and practicing gratitude.*
> Brene Brown

Something in Nature I feel grateful for

Unexpected goodness that happened today

_____
_____
_____
_____
_____
_____
_____
_____

I showed my thanks to someone today by....

_____
_____
_____
_____
_____
_____
_____
_____

Write down at least 3 things you feel gratitude for today.
As a personal challenge see if you can fill all the lines with things you feel thankful for.

_____
_____
_____
_____
_____
_____
_____
_____
_____
_____
_____
_____

> *At the age of 18, I made up my mind to never have another bad day in my life. I dove into a endless sea of gratitude from which I've never emerged.*
> *Patch Adams*

Something in Nature I feel grateful for

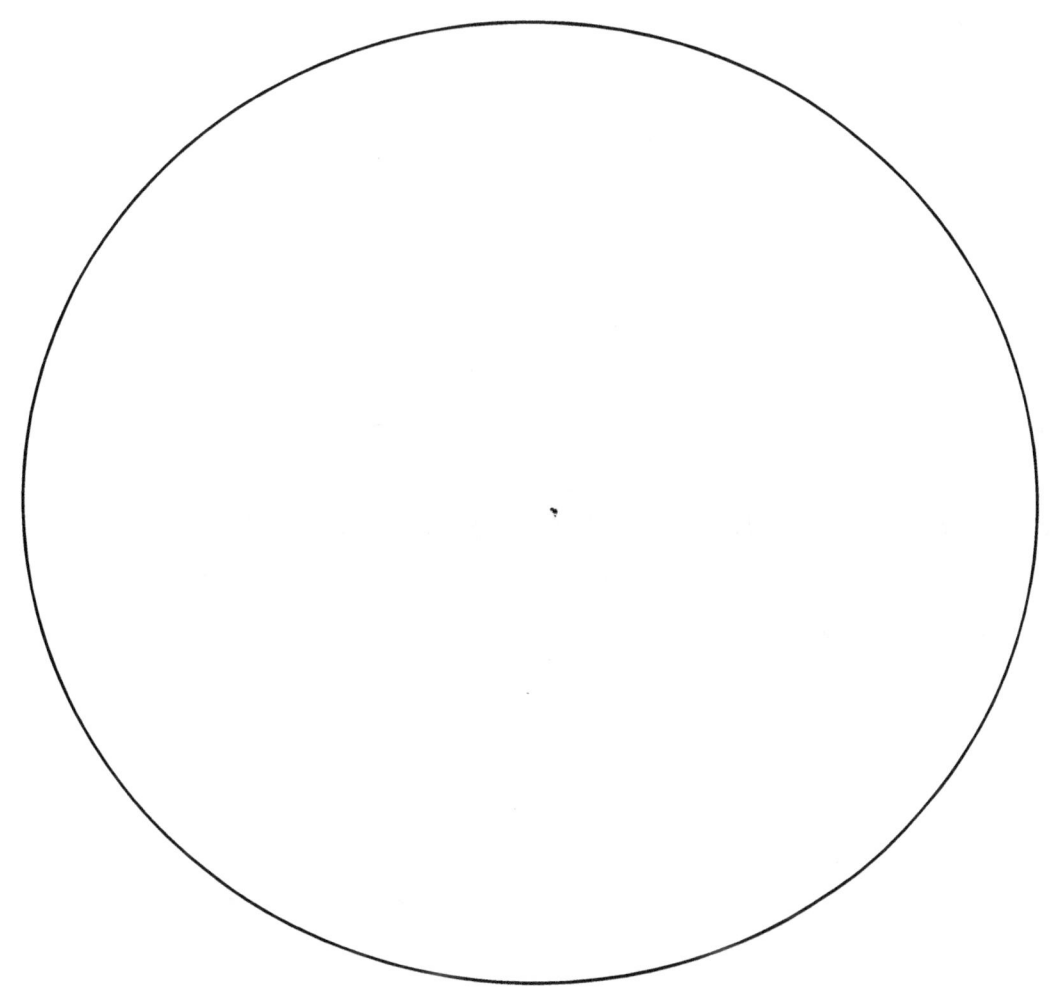

Unexpected goodness that happened today

_____
_____
_____
_____
_____
_____
_____
_____

I showed my thanks to someone today by....

_____
_____
_____
_____
_____
_____
_____

Write down at least 3 things you feel gratitude for today.
As a personal challenge see if you can fill all the lines with things you feel thankful for.

_____
_____
_____
_____
_____
_____
_____
_____
_____
_____
_____
_____

> *Never lose the childlike wonder. Show gratitude... Don't complain; just work harder... Never give up.*
> *Randy Pausch*

Something in Nature I feel grateful for

Unexpected goodness that happened today

_____
_____
_____
_____
_____
_____
_____
_____
_____

I showed my thanks to someone today by....

_____
_____
_____
_____
_____
_____
_____

Write down at least 3 things you feel gratitude for today.
As a personal challenge see if you can fill all the lines with things you feel thankful for.

_____
_____
_____
_____
_____
_____
_____
_____
_____
_____

> *Gratitude is a mark of a noble soul and a refined character. We like to be around those who are grateful.*
> *Joseph B. Wirthlin*

Something in Nature I feel grateful for

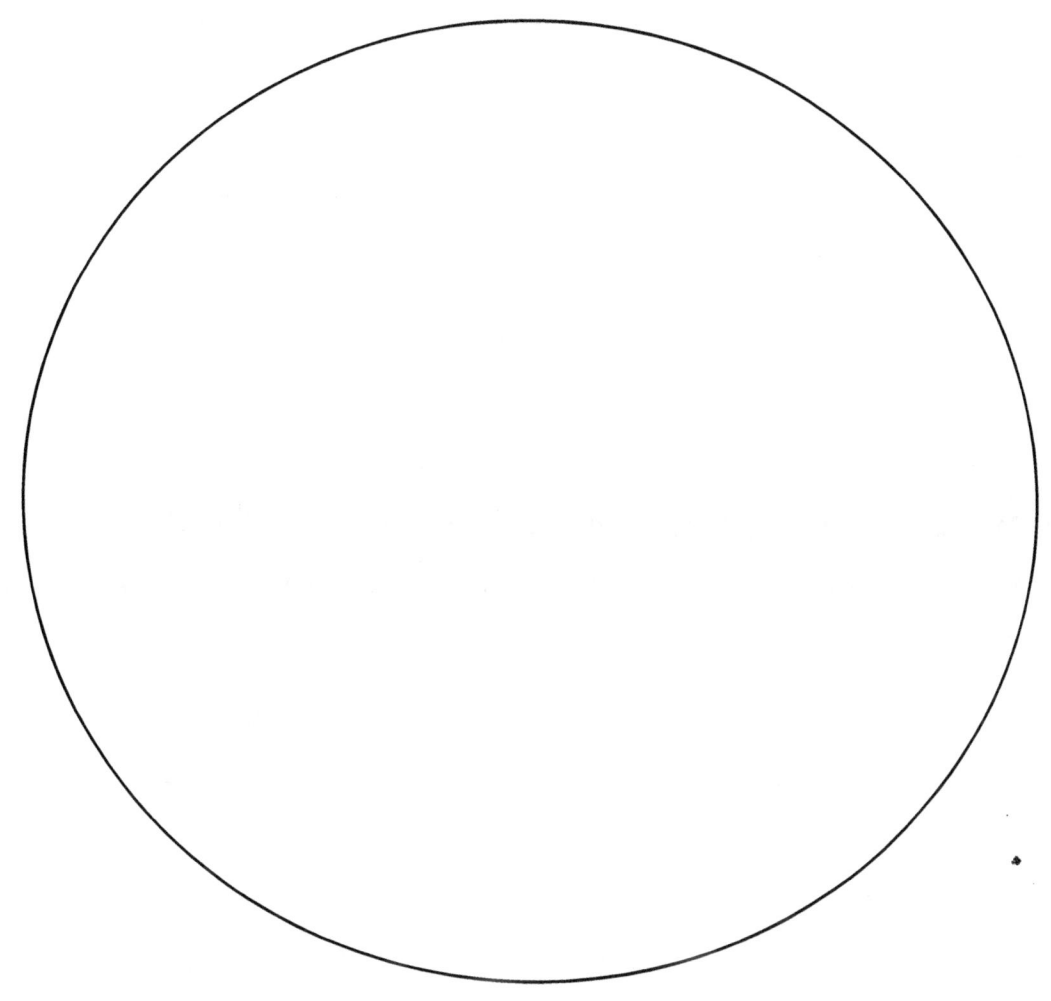

Unexpected goodness that happened today

_____
_____
_____
_____
_____
_____
_____
_____

I showed my thanks to someone today by....

_____
_____
_____
_____
_____
_____
_____
_____
_____

Write down at least 3 things you feel gratitude for today. As a personal challenge see if you can fill all the lines with things you feel thankful for.

_____
_____
_____
_____
_____
_____
_____
_____
_____
_____
_____
_____
_____
_____

> *Give yourself a gift of five minutes of contemplation in awe of everything you see around you. Go outside and turn your attention to the many miracles around you.*
> *Wayne Dyer*

Something in Nature I feel grateful for

Unexpected goodness that happened today

_____
_____
_____
_____
_____
_____
_____
_____

I showed my thanks to someone today by....

_____
_____
_____
_____
_____
_____
_____
_____

Write down at least 3 things you feel gratitude for today. As a personal challenge see if you can fill all the lines with things you feel thankful for.

_____
_____
_____
_____
_____
_____
_____
_____
_____
_____
_____
_____

> *Thankfulness is the beginning of gratitude. Gratitude is the completion of thankfulness. Thankfulness may consist merely of words. Gratitude is shown in acts.*
> *Henri Frederic Amiel*

Something in Nature I feel grateful for

Unexpected goodness that happened today

_____
_____
_____
_____
_____
_____
_____
_____

What a week! I love my gratitude journal.

Write down the difference you notice in your life as you have been focused on gratitude.

_____
_____
_____
_____
_____
_____
_____
_____
_____
_____
_____
_____
_____
_____
_____
_____
_____

> *Of all the characteristics needed for both a happy and morally decent life, none surpasses gratitude. Grateful people are happier, and grateful people are more morally decent.*
> *Dennis Prager*

**** 3 things I am grateful for today ****

_____
_____
_____
_____
_____

Dear _____
I never got to properly thank you. I would like to do that now........

_____
_____
_____
_____
_____
_____
_____
_____
_____
_____
_____
_____
_____
_____
_____
_____
_____
_____
_____
_____
_____

gratitude meter

| I feel the stirrings of something new | | my heart is so welled up with gratitude |

I showed my thanks to someone today by....
_____
_____
_____
_____
_____
_____
_____
_____

Write down at least 3 things you feel gratitude for today.
As a personal challenge see if you can fill all the lines with things you feel thankful for.

_____
_____
_____
_____
_____
_____

> *When it comes to life the critical thing is whether you take things for granted or take them with gratitude.*
> *Gilbert K. Chesterton*

Something in Nature I feel grateful for

Unexpected goodness that happened today

I showed my thanks to someone today by....

_____
_____
_____
_____
_____
_____
_____
_____

Write down at least 3 things you feel gratitude for today. As a personal challenge see if you can fill all the lines with things you feel thankful for.

_____
_____
_____
_____
_____
_____
_____
_____
_____
_____
_____
_____

> *The thankful heart opens our eyes to a multitude of blessings that continually surround us.*
> *James E. Faust*

Something in Nature I feel grateful for

Unexpected goodness that happened today

_____
_____
_____
_____
_____
_____
_____
_____
_____

I showed my thanks to someone today by....

_____
_____
_____
_____
_____
_____
_____
_____

Write down at least 3 things you feel gratitude for today.
As a personal challenge see if you can fill all the lines with things you feel thankful for.

_____
_____
_____
_____
_____
_____
_____
_____
_____
_____
_____
_____
_____

> *Gratitude is the inward feeling of kindness received. Thankfulness is the natural impulse to express that feeling. Thanksgiving is the following of that impulse.*
> *Henry Van Dyke*

Something in Nature I feel grateful for

Unexpected goodness that happened today

_____
_____
_____
_____
_____
_____
_____
_____

I showed my thanks to someone today by....

_____
_____
_____
_____
_____
_____
_____
_____

Write down at least 3 things you feel gratitude for today. As a personal challenge see if you can fill all the lines with things you feel thankful for.

_____
_____
_____
_____
_____
_____
_____
_____
_____
_____
_____
_____
_____
_____

> *It's wonderful to be grateful. To have that gratitude well out from deep within you and pour out in waves. Once you truly experience this, you will never want to give it up.*
> Srikumar Rao

Something in Nature I feel grateful for

Unexpected goodness that happened today

_____
_____
_____
_____
_____
_____
_____
_____
_____

I showed my thanks to someone today by....

_____
_____
_____
_____
_____
_____
_____
_____

Write down at least 3 things you feel gratitude for today.
As a personal challenge see if you can fill all the lines with things you feel thankful for.

_____
_____
_____
_____
_____
_____
_____
_____
_____
_____
_____

> *The discipline of gratitude is the explicit effort to acknowledge that all I am and have is given to me as a gift of love, a gift to be celebrated with joy.*
> *Henri Nouwen*

Something in Nature I feel grateful for

Unexpected goodness that happened today

_____
_____
_____
_____
_____
_____
_____
_____

I showed my thanks to someone today by....

_____
_____
_____
_____
_____
_____
_____
_____

Write down at least 3 things you feel gratitude for today.
As a personal challenge see if you can fill all the lines with things you feel thankful for.

_____
_____
_____
_____
_____
_____
_____
_____
_____
_____
_____
_____
_____

> *Nature's beauty is a gift that cultivates appreciation and gratitude.*
> Louie Schwartzberg

Something in Nature I feel grateful for

Unexpected goodness that happened today

_____
_____
_____
_____
_____
_____
_____
_____
_____

What a week! I love my gratitude journal.

Write down the difference you notice in your life as you have been focused on gratitude.

___

> *Giving is an expression of gratitude for our blessings.*
> *Laura Arrillaga-Andreessen*

**** 3 things I am grateful for today ****

___

Dear _____
I never got to properly thank you. I would like to do that now........

_____

gratitude meter

| I feel the stirrings of something new | | my heart is so welled up with gratitude |

I showed my thanks to someone today by....

Write down at least 3 things you feel gratitude for today.
As a personal challenge see if you can fill all the lines with things you feel thankful for.

> *I have had friends who have acted kindly towards me, and it has been my good fortune to have it in my power to give them substantial proofs of my gratitude.*
> *Giacomo Casanova*

Something in Nature I feel grateful for

Unexpected goodness that happened today

I showed my thanks to someone today by....

_____
_____
_____
_____
_____
_____
_____
_____

Write down at least 3 things you feel gratitude for today.
As a personal challenge see if you can fill all the lines with things you feel thankful for.

_____
_____
_____
_____
_____
_____
_____
_____
_____
_____
_____
_____
_____

> *Gratitude is riches.*
> *Complaint is poverty.*
> *Doris Day*

Something in Nature I feel grateful for

Unexpected goodness that happened today

_____
_____
_____
_____
_____
_____
_____
_____

I showed my thanks to someone today by....

_____
_____
_____
_____
_____
_____
_____
_____

Write down at least 3 things you feel gratitude for today. As a personal challenge see if you can fill all the lines with things you feel thankful for.

_____
_____
_____
_____
_____
_____
_____
_____
_____
_____
_____
_____

> *Let us swell with gratitude and allow it to overwhelm us. It isn't as cliche as we make it; life truly is short. Let's spend it all lavishly wallowing in gratitude.*
> *Grace Gealey*

Something in Nature I feel grateful for

Unexpected goodness that happened today

I showed my thanks to someone today by....

_____
_____
_____
_____
_____
_____
_____

Write down at least 3 things you feel gratitude for today. As a personal challenge see if you can fill all the lines with things you feel thankful for.

_____
_____
_____
_____
_____
_____
_____
_____
_____
_____
_____

> *Fill the earth with your songs of gratitude.*
> *Charles Spurgeon*

Something in Nature I feel grateful for

Unexpected goodness that happened today

_____
_____
_____
_____
_____
_____
_____
_____

I showed my thanks to someone today by....

_____
_____
_____
_____
_____
_____
_____
_____

Write down at least 3 things you feel gratitude for today.
As a personal challenge see if you can fill all the lines with things you feel thankful for.

_____
_____
_____
_____
_____
_____
_____
_____
_____
_____
_____
_____

> *I'm just thankful for everything, all the blessings in my life, trying to stay that way. I think that's the best way to start your day and finish your day. It keeps everything in perspective.*
> *Tim Tebow*

Something in Nature I feel grateful for

Unexpected goodness that happened today

I showed my thanks to someone today by....

_____
_____
_____
_____
_____
_____
_____
_____

Write down at least 3 things you feel gratitude for today.
As a personal challenge see if you can fill all the lines with things you feel thankful for.

_____
_____
_____
_____
_____
_____
_____
_____
_____
_____
_____
_____

> *When I started counting my blessings, my whole life turned around.*
> *Willie Nelson*

Something in Nature I feel grateful for

Unexpected goodness that happened today

_____
_____
_____
_____
_____
_____
_____
_____

What a week! I love my gratitude journal.

Write down the difference you notice in your life as you have been focused on gratitude.

___
___
___
___
___
___
___
___
___
___
___
___
___
___

> *When you rise in the morning, give thanks for the light, for your life, for your strength. Give thanks for your food and for the joy of living. If you see no reason to give thanks, the fault lies in yourself.*

**** 3 things I am grateful for today ****

___
___
___
___
___

Dear _____
I never got to properly thank you. I would like to do that now........

_____
_____
_____
_____
_____
_____
_____
_____
_____
_____
_____
_____
_____
_____
_____
_____
_____
_____
_____
_____

gratitude meter

| I feel the stirrings of something new | | my heart is so welled up with gratitude |

gratitude goodies, new discoveries, and notes

gratitude goodies, new discoveries, and notes

gratitude goodies, new discoveries, and notes

gratitude goodies, new discoveries, and notes

gratitude goodies, new discoveries, and notes

Available Now
From Uiri Press

The I Am So Happy journal is a 46 day exploration into what makes you happy.

By Sky Hawk

ISBN 978-0-9979051-0-6

The I am So Peaceful journal is an expedition into what brings peace into your life and how to keep it there.

By Sky Hawk

ISBN 978-0-9979051-2-0

The I am So Prosperous journal is an adventure into bringing success and prosperity into your life.

By Sky Hawk

ISBN 978-0-9979051-3-7

About the Author

Sky Hawk is an author, artist, nature lover, successful entrepreneur, healer, and mother. She is the creator of her life, the I Am So series, herbal tracking journals, and much more. She helps people feel the love in themselves and is a spreader of joy.
Visit her and follow along the journey
website: SkyTheAuthor.com
facebook: @skyhawkauthor
instagram: sky_hawk_author

www.ingramcontent.com/pod-product-compliance
Lightning Source LLC
Chambersburg PA
CBHW060457300426
44113CB00016B/2624